TRAVEL SCIENCE

SCIENCE 24/7

ANIMAL SCIENCE

CAR SCIENCE

COMPUTER SCIENCE

ENVIRONMENTAL SCIENCE

FASHION SCIENCE

FOOD SCIENCE

HEALTH SCIENCE

MUSIC SCIENCE

PHOTO SCIENCE

SPORTS SCIENCE

TRAVEL SCIENCE

SCIENCE 24/7

TRAVEL SCIENCE

JANE P. GARDNER

SCIENCE CONSULTANT:
RUSS LEWIN
SCIENCE AND MATH EDUCATOR

Mason Crest

Mason Crest
450 Parkway Drive, Suite D
Broomall, PA 19008
www.masoncrest.com

Series ISBN: 978-1-4222-3404-4
Hardback ISBN: 978-1-4222-3415-0
EBook ISBN: 978-1-4222-8499-5

First printing
1 3 5 7 9 8 6 4 2

Produced by Shoreline Publishing Group LLC
Santa Barbara, California
Editorial Director: James Buckley Jr.
Designer: Patty Kelley
www.shorelinepublishing.com
Cover photo: Dreamstime.com/Vadimgozhda

Library of Congress Cataloging-in-Publication Data
Gardner, Jane P., author.
        Travel science / by Jane P. Gardner; science consultant, Russ Lewin, Science and Math Educator.
        pages cm. -- (Science 24/7)
Audience: Grades 9 to 12
Includes bibliographical references and index.   ISBN 978-1-4222-3415-0 (hardback) -- ISBN 978-1-4222-3404-4 (series) -- ISBN 978-1-4222-8499-5 (ebook) 1. Air travel--Miscellanea--Juvenile literature. 2. Space flight--Miscellanea--Juvenile literature. 3. Transportation--Miscellanea--Juvenile literature. I. Title.
HE152.G32 2016
910--dc23
                                2015005000

IMPORTANT NOTICE
The science experiments, activities, and information described in this publication are for educational use only. The publisher is not responsible for any direct, indirect, incidental or consequential damages as a result of the uses or misuses of the techniques and information within.

Contents

KEY ICONS TO LOOK FOR

 Words to Understand: These words with their easy-to-understand definitions will increase the reader's understanding of the text, while building vocabulary skills.

 Sidebars: This boxed material within the main text allows readers to build knowledge, gain insights, explore possibilities, and broaden their perspectives by weaving together additional information to provide realistic and holistic perspectives.

 Series Glossary of Key Terms: This back-of-the-book glossary contains terminology used throughout this series. Words found here increase the reader's ability to read and comprehend higher-level books and articles in this field.

INTRODUCTION

Science. Ugh! Is this the class you have to sit through in order to get to the cafeteria for lunch? Or, yeah! This is my favorite class! Whether you look forward to science or dread it, you can't escape it. Science is all around us all the time.

What do you think of when you think about science? People in lab coats peering anxiously through microscopes while scribbling notes? Giant telescopes scanning the universe for signs of life? Submersibles trolling the dark, cold, and lonely world of the deepest ocean? Yes, these are all science and things that scientists do to learn more about our planet, outer space, and the human body. But we are all scientists. Even you.

Science is about asking questions. Why do I have to eat my vegetables? Why does the sun set in the west? Why do cats purr and dogs bark? Why am I warmer when I wear a black jacket than when I wear a white one? These are all great questions. And these questions can be the start of something big . . . the start of scientific discovery.

1. **Observe:** Ask questions. What do you see in the world around you that you don't understand? What do you wish you knew more about? Remember, there is always more than one solution to a problem. This is the starting point for scientists—and it can be the starting point for you, too!

   Enrique took a slice of bread out of the package and discovered there was mold on it. "Again?" he complained. "This is the second time this all-natural bread I bought turned moldy before I could finish it. I wonder why."

2. **Research:** Find out what you can about the observation you have made. The more information you learn about your observation, the better you will understand which questions really need to be answered.

   Enrique researched the term "all-natural" as it applied to his bread. He discovered that it meant that no preservatives were used. Some breads contain preservatives, which are used to "maintain freshness." Enrique wondered if it was the lack of preservatives that was allowing his bread to grow mold.

3. **Predict:** Consider what might happen if you were to design an experiment based on your research. What do you think you would find?

   Enrique thought that maybe it was the lack of preservatives in his bread that was causing the mold. He predicted that bread containing preservatives would last longer than "all-natural" breads.

4. **Develop a Hypothesis:** A hypothesis is a possible answer or solution to a scientific problem. Sometimes, they are written as an "if-then" statement. For example, "If I get a good night's sleep, then I will do well on the test tomorrow." This is not a fact; there is no guarantee that the hypothesis is correct. But it is a statement that can be tested with an experiment. And then, if necessary, revised once the experiment has been done.

Enrique thinks that he knows what is going on. He figures that the preservatives in the bread are what keeps it from getting moldy. His working hypothesis is, "If bread contains preservatives, it will not grow mold." He is now ready to test his hypothesis.

5. **Design an Experiment:** An experiment is designed to test a hypothesis. It is important when designing an experiment to look at all the variables. Variables are the factors that will change in the experiment. Some variables will be independent—these won't change. Others are dependent and will change as the experiment progresses. A control is necessary, too. This is a constant throughout the experiment against which results can be compared.

Enrique plans his experiment. He chooses two slices of his bread, and two slices of the bread with preservatives. He uses a small kitchen scale to ensure that the slices are approximately the same weight. He places a slice of each on the windowsill where they will receive the same amount of sunlight. He places the other two slices in a dark cupboard. He checks on his bread every day for a week. He finds that his bread gets mold in both places while the bread with preservatives starts to grow a little mold in the sunshine but none in the cupboard.

6. **Revise the hypothesis:** Sometimes the result of your experiment will show that the original hypothesis is incorrect. That is okay! Science is all about taking risks, making mistakes, and learning from them. Rewriting a hypothesis after examining the data is what this is all about.

Enrique realized it may be more than the preservatives that prevents mold. Keeping the bread out of the sunlight and in a dark place will help preserve it, even without preservatives. He has decided to buy smaller quantities of bread now, and keep it in the cupboard.

This book has activities for you to try at the end of each chapter. They are meant to be fun, and teach you a little bit at the same time. Sometimes, you'll be asked to design your own experiment. Think back to Enrique's experience when you start designing your own. And remember—science is about being curious, being patient, and not being afraid of saying you made a mistake. There are always other experiments to be done!

1
AIRPLANES

Mei sat back in her seat as the airplane taxied down the runway. She could see the lights from the airport terminal flickering in the distance as they made their final lap before take off. She looked over at her younger brother, Hayato, sitting next to her.

"Looking forward to going home?"

Hayato looked up from his phone, where he was playing a game. "Not really. I had a great time in Japan. And this is basically the end of summer vacation. Back to school." He frowned as he turned his attention back to his game.

Mei settled into her seat as the plane began to pick up speed. Her parents were seated a few rows ahead of them and her mom turned around to give them the thumbs up sign.

Mei and Hayato looked out the window as the plane sped down the runway, then lifted up off the ground and rose steadily into the air. A couple of minutes later, they heard the wheels being retracted into the bottom of the plane and they released a breath that they didn't even realize they were holding.

Grabbing the magazine in the seat pocket, Mei said, "Let's see if we can find out a little more about this plane. It is pretty amazing that it can get us over the Pacific all the way home to Chicago."

The plane they were riding in was a Boeing 777. Tip to tip, the wingspan was 212.7 feet (64 m) long while the entire plane was 209 feet (63 m) long. Once the plane reached its cruising altitude, it would travel at a rate of 560 miles (901 km) per hour. With plenty of fuel, the plane could travel 10,375 miles (16,697 km).

"Well," Mei said, "looks like we'll make it. According to this it is just over 6,000 miles (9,656 km) to Chicago. We'll have plenty of fuel left over. Even after our a thirteen-hour flight."

"Ugh. Thirteen hours. That is so long," Hayato rolled his eyes. "It is still amazing that this big hunk of metal can get all the way across the ocean."

"I know! Just like a bird."

Hayato looked at her. "Just like a bird?"

Mei nodded. "Yes, the physical properties of flight are very similar for a bird and a plane. The wings of a plane work on the same idea as the wings of a bird. They use the concept of lift." Pointing out the window, Mei continued, "Look at the shape of that wing. See how the top part is curved and the bottom is pretty much flat?"

Hayato said, "Well, I can't really see the bottom of the wing from up here, but okay."

"This creates a difference in pressure," continued Mei. "The air flowing over the wing will move faster over the top of the wing; this creates less pressure on top, and more pressure on the bottom, which lifts the wing."

"That's right," Hayato conceded. "I also read somewhere that there are basically four forces of flight. There is lift, which you have mentioned. But there is also drag. Drag occurs when a solid moves through a liquid. This is why your hand feels heavy when you run it through the water. Drag slows the plane down, as it flies through the air."

Mei added, "But something has to counteract the drag. Or else we wouldn't go forward."

"Yep. And that is thrust," Hayato said.

Words to Understand

drag the force opposite to the motion of an object through the air

gravity the force that pulls objects toward the ground

lift the force that acts to raise a wing or an airfoil

thrust the force placed on an object by expelling gas or mass in one direction, causing the object to move in the opposite direction

"This is the work that the engines do to propel us forward," she continued.

"There must be a force, then, to counterbalance the lift I was talking about," said Mei.

"Of course there is. That's **gravity**!" Hayato said.

Mei looked out the window. "That's a lot of forces that all have to work together to get us up in the air and on our way home."

Sir Isaac Newton and Flight

Sir Isaac Newton died nearly 150 years before Orville and Wilbur Wright built the first working airplane in 1903. But it was Newton's laws of motion that explained how and why flight is possible. His laws said the following:

- An object that is at rest will remain at rest until an outside force acts upon it. If an object is in motion, then it will stay in motion and not change direction unless it is acted upon by an outside force.
- The harder an object is pushed, the farther and faster it will move.
- If an object is pushed in one direction, there is resistance on that object working in the opposite direction.

These three laws of motion led to the understanding that the four forces of lift, drag, gravity, and thrust all must act together to make flight possible.

Try It Yourself

Make your own paper airplane.

Materials:
- drinking straws
- tape
- heavyweight paper, cardboard or thin balsa wood

1. Decide if you want to make a paper airplane that stays aloft the longest or one that glides the greatest distance.

2. Check out the Internet or other resources to find pictures of the type of plane you'd like to make. Take special note of the shape of the wings and other features that might be on the plane.

3. Use the materials listed to make a paper airplane. Be sure to keep in mind the basics behind the idea of lift.

4. If possible, toss your paper airplane along the length of the gymnasium or auditorium to observe its flight patterns. Make adjustments to your design as needed.

2
SHIPS

Hayato took out a book about pirates he was reading. "I am glad we didn't live back then. Can you imagine how long it would take to cross the Pacific Ocean in one of these?" he said, pointing to an old wooden sailboat.

Flipping through the pages he continued, "Here's something I really don't understand. How can a boat built to float on the water, sink?" He pointed to a picture of a shipwreck on the bottom of the ocean floor. "I know the whole story about the Titanic hitting an iceberg and all, but if it floated once, why would it sink?"

"We learned about this last year in physics class," Mei explained. "It has to do with **buoyancy**."

"What?"

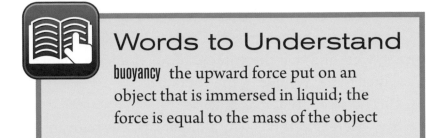
Mei explained, "Buoyant forces are sort of like gravity. Gravity pulls everything down toward Earth, right? Water, and other fluids actually exert their own force—a buoyant force. It's an upward force on an object. It acts in the opposite direction of gravity, making things feel lighter."

Hayato caught on, "Which is why I feel lighter in the pool!"

"Exactly." Just then the flight attendant came around with the drink cart. "May I please have a cup of water with no ice?" Mei asked. "Thank you."

Mei reached into her carry-on bag and pulled out an empty pill bottle. She placed five pennies inside. She turned to her brother and said, "What do you think will happen when I drop this into the cup of water?"

"Duh . . . it'll sink."

"Alright. Let's see." She dropped it in and the bottle sank. Some of the water spilled over the top of the cup.

Mei cleaned up the spilt water with a napkin and took the pennies out of the canister. She refilled the cup of water to its original level. She held up the empty canister and said, "What if I put this in?"

Hayato looked less sure this time. "I think it will . . . float?"

"Let's see." She dropped the empty canister into the cup. It floated with just part of it under water. Some water spilled over the top, but not as much as before.

Mei cleaned up the mess again. "Ta-dah! Did you see it?"

"See what?"

"I just showed you how a boat floats! That was Archimedes' principle at work. He was an ancient Greek mathematician who came up with formulas and ideas on how to explain things."

Mei continued, "Did you see me clean up the water each time?" Hayato nodded.

"There was a bigger mess the time the canister sank than the time it floated. If we could measure it, we'd find that the volume of water displaced, or pushed out, by the canister each time was equal to the volume of the container."

Hayato said, "That makes sense."

"So," Mei said, "this is why a ship floats. The buoyant force equals the weight of the fluid that was displaced. So a really big, heavy object, like a ship, will float because it has a larger buoyant force. A ship's hull is pretty big; the volume of water it displaces is significant enough to keep it afloat."

A Great Greek

Archimedes lived in ancient Greece from 287 B.C.E. until his death in 212 B.C.E. He is credited with having been a mathematician, physicist, engineer, inventor, and astronomer. He calculated the formulas for the area of a circle and the surface area and volume of a sphere. He also calculated an accurate approximation of the value of pi and invented machines such as the screw pump and the compound pulley. His inventions were used to help protect his home city of Syracuse from invasion. All did not go as planned, however, when the Romans attacked Syracuse in a two-year battle. Archimedes was killed during the siege by a Roman solider, even though there were strict orders that he not be harmed.

Try It Yourself

Ships are made of steel. How on earth do they float? Try this quick activity to see how the shape of the boat's hull can make all the difference.

Materials:
- ball of clay—about the size of a golf ball
- paper towels
- sink full of water or large clear container filled with water

1. Roll the clay into a ball. Drop it into the water. What happens?

2. Dry the clay ball with a paper towel and shape it into a "boat." It should look like a shallow cup with a small keel at the bottom of the boat. Place that in the water. What happens?

3. What do you think will happen if you add water to the boat? Write your prediction here.

4. Try it. Add water to the boat. Does it sink or float? Why do you think this happened?

3
TIME ZONES

As the flight attendant made her way back down the aisle with the drink cart, Hayato looked up. "What time is it anyway?"

Looking at her watch, Mei said, "Right now, right here in this plane, my watch says it is 10 AM. We've been flying for about three hours now."

Hayato shook his head. "This time thing really confuses me. What time is it in Japan right now?"

Mei admitted, "I haven't changed my watch yet. It is 10 AM in Tokyo."

"And what time is it in Chicago again?"

Mei smiled as she knew what his reaction was going to be. "In Chicago, it is 8 PM last night."

"Ahhh!" Hayato yelped good-naturedly. "I can't take it! Show me how that is possible."

Mei pointed to the map that was in the magazine. "Here, look at this. There are 24 time zones on Earth." Mei stared at the map. "I think we need to back up a little bit first."

Taking out a piece of paper and a colored pencil she had in her bag, she continued, "Earth can be split up in different ways. There are lines of **latitude** which go around the planet, north and south of the equator." Mei drew this on the sheet of paper. "And there are lines of **longitude** which run from east to west and stretch from the North Pole to the South Pole."

Mei continued with her sketch. "Every point on the planet has its own special location, which you find by its latitude and its longitude. But this isn't really what we are talking about. There are a total of 360 degrees of longitude. That is, 180 degrees to the east and 180 degrees to the west."

Hayato interrupted, "To the east or west of what?"

"The **prime meridian**. This is an imaginary line of longitude that runs through Greenwich, England, right here," she said pointing to the map. "If you started at the prime meridian, which has a value of 0 degrees latitude, and went west, you'd move along the degrees of latitude and in that direction, your watch should be moved to an earlier time. So if it was 10 AM on the prime meridian, then it would be 9 AM here," she said, pointing to a spot on the map.

"And," Mei continued, "if you go east from there, then it is later. It would be 11 AM here. As you move west around the globe, you 'pick up' time. As you move east, you 'lose' it. Of course, the time is not lost. Time continues at the same pace. What changes is the name of the time of day."

"Okay, smarty. Then how can it be Tuesday here and Monday at home?"

Mei picked up the map again. "About halfway around the world from the prime meridian is what is called the International Date Line. This means that at any given point it is two different days, depending on where you on Earth. That helps with such practical issues as making sure to have noon during the daylight hours and midnight during the night time hours. If you did not change the time of the clock as you moved around the Earth, no one would be able to schedule or plan anything. Imagine if everyone decided on their own what 'o'clock' it was in their area."

Mei went on to explain that while the lines of latitude and longitude are a general guide to the time zones, they do not follow them exactly. In fact, a map of the time zones shows that some of the 24 sections have very jagged edges as they bend out or in to include some islands or countries.

Words to Understand

latitude invisible lines of measurement that circle the Earth parallel to the Equator and define distance from the Equator

longitude invisible lines of measurement that encircle the Earth north and south

prime meridian measured at 0° longitude, this line passes through Greenwich, England, and from it all other longitude lines are measured

The time zones were laid out so that, when possible, a whole nation was on the same time zone.

"Look at the map here in this magazine," Mei went on. "The time zone changes between Tunisia and Libya, for example, or between Peru and Bolivia. Larger countries, however, can have many time zones. The United States has four, while Russia has eleven!"

"That's too many clocks for me," Hayato laughed. "I think I'll just make sure my alarm clock is set to get me up in the morning . . . no matter what time it is!"

A Change in the Ocean

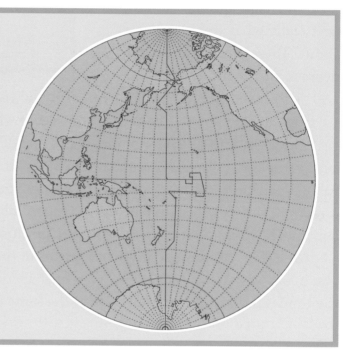

The International Date Line lies in the middle of the Pacific Ocean, roughly following the 180-degree meridian line. This means that the change from one day to another is always done on a plane or ship. A good thing, too; it would be tough to change the day as you drove back and forth to school each day!

Try it Yourself

Four...three...two...one...Happy New Year! Every year, thousands gather to watch the crystal ball in New York City's Times Square drop, ringing in a new year. But in some places it has already been January 1 for hours. And some places are in the middle of the day on December 31. Where would you have to be to be one of the first to ring in the new year? Or to hold on to the old year the longest?

Materials:
- world map with time zones
- watch or clock

1. Find your home on the map. In which time zone do you live?

2. Suppose you were watching television on New Year's Eve and watched the ball drop at 11:59 PM in Times Square. What time would it be where you live?

3. Where on Earth is the last place that would be 11:59 PM on December 31?

4. Where is the first place on Earth to be 12:01 AM, January 1?

5. Suppose you flew on a plane from Sydney, Australia, to Santiago, Chile, on December 31. Not worrying about the time it takes to travel, what day would it be when you landed in Chile? What if you immediately boarded a plane and flew back to Australia. What day would it be?

4
JET LAG

A few more hours into the flight, Mei and Hayato's father came back to check on them. By this time, many of the other passengers had shut their overhead lights off and closed the window shades.

"You two should really try to get some sleep, you know," he said.

"Really, Dad? It feels like it is early afternoon," Mei said.

"You are right, if we were still in Tokyo. But it is midnight in Chicago. Don't you remember how we all felt tired after our flight to Japan, but also jet lagged? Jet lag is always worse when you travel east than it is when you travel west. This is going to be a bigger deal for us this time."

Mei sighed, "Okay, we'll try to get some sleep."

Patting her on the shoulder, her father pointed out, "Then you'd better shut off that light and turn off your games for now."

Curling his feet underneath him on the seat, Hayato said,

"Mei, remind me again what jet lag is. I forgot. I was so excited about being in Japan that I didn't even know I was tired."

The woman sitting in the window seat next to them spoke up, "I know the answer to that question."

Mei was relieved. "Great. Can you tell him? I forget the actual cause."

The woman smiled. "Jet lag is an upset in your body's natural **circadian rhythm**. That is like your body's internal clock. Flying across many time zones will throw your body off. Your body feels like it is in one time zone while the clock says you are in another."

Mei nodded. "Right. We know that when it was 10 AM on Tuesday in Tokyo it was 8 PM Monday night at home in Chicago. I guess our brains really won't know what to expect when we get home."

"It's because we are traveling so fast over so many time zones," the woman continued. "Jet lag wasn't an issue in the past when it took weeks to cross the Pacific on a boat. But flying from one continent to another in a matter of hours is rough on the system."

It's 10 in the morning in Tokyo . . . and 8 in the evening in Chicago.

Melatonin

Melatonin is a hormone produced in the brain. It helps control your natural circadian rhythm—that is the natural sleep–wake cycle. Melatonin is produced naturally in animals, plants, and microbes. Sometimes, a melatonin supplement can be taken to help control sleep problems. The use of melatonin as a sleep aid should be discussed with a doctor.

"I didn't feel that bad when we landed in Japan. Maybe I was just so excited to be there," said Hayato.

The woman agreed. "That is a possibility. But it turns out that flying to the west is easier than flying eastward. You gained hours when you flew to Japan. Your body can adjust to that more easily."

"Yikes, and now we are losing time flying east. This could be rough."

The woman agreed with him. "There are a few things you can do which will make the transition easier. Right now, for example, you want to make sure you have plenty to drink on the plane. Staying hydrated is important. When you get home, soak up some sunshine the first morning home. That might help. Try to get back into a regular routine with your normal bedtime. That can help. And get some exercise."

"That sounds like good advice. Thanks."

The woman replied, "Now, I think your father had a good point. We should try to get a little sleep while on the plane. It can't hurt."

Try it Yourself

How does light affect your sleep? Design an experiment that you think would work. Suppose you were asked to design an experiment to figure out if sleeping with the light on interrupted your sleep. Or try an experiment about the sleep patterns of people who work the night shift. What would your experiment look like?

Suggested Materials:
- paper
- pencil

1. Devise your hypothesis.

2. What is your procedure? List the steps.

3. How many trials will you do? What is your controlled variable? Your independent variable?

4. Predict what your results will be.

5. Explain what you think you would see.

6. Draw a conclusion.

Note: With your grown-ups' permission, you might want to conduct your experiment on a weekend or a school vacation. Was your prediction correct?

5
THE CORIOLIS EFFECT

Mei thanked the woman next to her for helping out. "Where are you flying from?"

"I was in Australia for two months and I'm headed home to Miami."

Hayato chimed in "Wow. Australia. The Land Down Under, with kangaroos and koalas and dingoes."

The woman smiled. "Yes, it was an amazing trip."

Hayato looked over at her. "You know, I heard that the water runs down the toilet the opposite direction in Australia. Is that true?"

"Hayato! That's not appropriate." Mei scolded him.

The woman laughed, "Actually it is a very good question. And, no, it doesn't."

Hayato shook his head. "I was pretty sure I heard that somewhere."

"What you heard is a very common misconception. It is all based on the **Coriolis effect**," explained the woman.

"The Corio-who what the heck?" Hayato shot back.

"The Coriolis effect. Everything—air, water, baseballs—feels the effect of Earth's rotation on its axis. Objects in the northern hemisphere are turned to the right relative to Earth's surface,

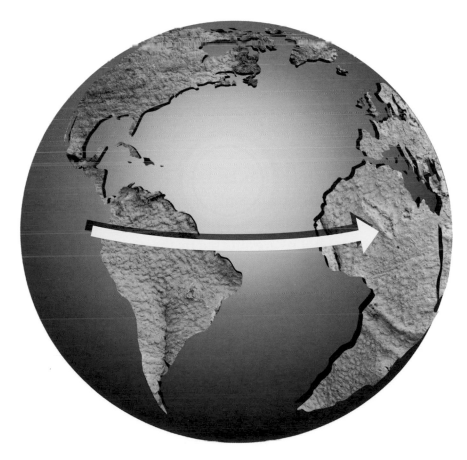

Right now, you and the Earth are spinning from the west to the east.

25

Tornadoes and the Coriolis Effect

Tornadoes in the northern hemisphere spin in a counterclockwise direction while those in the southern hemisphere spin clockwise. However, this is not directly the result of the Coriolis effect. Tornadoes are too small, and too short-lived, to feel the full impact of the Coriolis effect.

while objects in the southern hemisphere are turned to the left. Which is why you heard that the water runs down a drain in the opposite direction in the southern hemisphere."

"But if Earth's rotation makes things move in a particular direction, then why doesn't the water flow down the drain in that direction?" wondered Mei.

"There just isn't enough water. The effect is very subtle on that scale," the woman explained. "But rockets and sometimes airplanes have to take the Coriolis effect into consideration."

She went on, "Suppose a rocket was fired from the North Pole straight south. It would be aiming for the middle of Kansas." She pointed to the map that the kids had been looking at before. "And to make things simpler, say it takes one hour for the rocket to go that distance. Where will the rocket land?"

Hayato looked at the map. "Uh, over here somewhere?" he asked, pointing in Nevada.

"Exactly! The rocket would land to the west of its target. People who shoot off rockets need to take this into consideration."

Mei understood. "So if I tried to shoot a rocket from the South Pole to the tip of Africa, the rocket would land in the southern Atlantic ocean!"

"Right you are. The Coriolis effect has a significant impact on the winds on Earth, too. Massive storms like hurricanes and typhoons are affected by these phenomena."

Try It Yourself

How does the Coriolis effect impact the movement of air on Earth? Sometimes the best way to find out is to watch it happen yourself.

Materials:
- poster board
- markers, 2 colors

1. Suppose you were to draw, or attempt to draw, a straight line from the bottom of the page to the top of the page while the paper was rotating in a clockwise direction. What do you think would happen? Write your prediction here.

2. With at least two other people, try this. One person should loosely hold down the center of the paper by placing their finger or a capped marker in the center of the paper. The paper should be able to spin, but it should not slide around.

3. A second person will spin the paper in a clockwise direction at a steady rate. Not too fast, and not too slow.

4. The last person will use another marker and attempt to draw a straight line from the center to the outer edge of the paper, while the paper is spinning.

5. Try this and see what happens.

6. Explain what happened. Did this model movement in the northern or southern hemisphere? How do you know?

6
SPACE TRAVEL

Mei leaned back in her seat and opened the window shade. She could see the stars out of the window, twinkling in the distance. Turning to Hayato, she said, "Would you want to fly into space if you could?"

Hayato leaned over to look at the stars. "To leave Earth, fly out there for a while, and then come home? I'd go as long as I could come home again."

"Well, we'd all be a lot older when you got home, you know."

"Oh, I know. But I'd be young and I could go on to tell everyone about my experiences and visit you in the rest home."

Mei glared at him. "Why would I be old but you won't be? If you are gone for ten years then we'd both age ten years."

Hayato shook his head. "Nope. I read about it a while ago. It's called the twin paradox. It's all about space and time, you know, special **relativity**."

"Yes, I learned all about Albert Einstein and space and time, too, you know."

"Then you know what I am talking about! If one twin got

in a super-fast space ship and went almost the speed of light to a star out there and then came back here, that twin would be younger than the other would be when they returned. The fancy term for it is time dilation.

"That just means that when two different frames of reference move differently, then they experience time differently. If I go to the distant galaxy then I am moving in a different frame of reference than you are here on Earth. If the whole trip takes me five years, I experienced five years of life on my reference frame."

Mei slowly said, "And . . . then I would maybe experience fifteen years of my life here on Earth within my frame of reference."

Hayato clapped his hands. "Yes! Scientists who talk about this have actual numbers and dates and years that they can use. But that is the basics of it."

Mei shook her head. "I still think this is hard to get my brain around."

The German scientist Albert Einstein won the 1921 Nobel Prize in Physics for his work describing how space and time relate.

Speed of Light

The speed of light is approximately 186,282 miles (300,000 km) per second. At this rate, it takes just about eight minutes for light from the Sun to travel the 93 million miles (150 million km) to Earth. This means you are looking into the past every time you look out at a sunny day.

Try It Yourself

Albert Einstein was one of the most influential scientists of all time. Suppose you had the opportunity to travel back in time to meet with him and interview him for your school's blog. What would you ask him? What could you tell him about our views on science today that is a direct result of his contributions? Prepare well for your interview—he would surely have a lot of questions for you, too.

Materials:
- pen
- pencil
- Internet access

1. Read about Einstein's theories of relativity. Which would you like to question him about?

2. Write out the questions you would ask him about his theory.

3. List 2–4 examples of how this theory is used today and the current scientific thinking about his theories. How have they changed since Einstein's death?

4. How have physics and astronomy and scientific thinking in general changed as a result of Einstein's ideas? What would you tell him about that?

7
CHALLENGES
IN SPACE

"If I could travel to space," Mei continued, "I would want to work on the International Space Station. Some of the experiments that they are doing up there are amazing."

"Yeah? Like what?"

"I just read about how images taken from the International Space Station and observations made by the scientists there are helping scientists back on Earth track changes to the ecosystems as a result of natural events like volcanic eruptions, earthquakes, and massive hurricanes."

"That is pretty neat. What else do they do up there?"

Mei settled into her discussion. She had done a lot of research on the topic. "There have been a ton of health-related experiments and studies done up there. The astronauts on the space station are in a unique situation. Their expeditions usually last three to six months. Studies on the effects of life on the space station are helping scientists determine if longer space flights, such as a trip to Mars, would be possible for humans."

"How long would it take to get to Mars?"

"I think about six months."

Hayato thought some more. "And if it took six months to get there, they would want to spend some time there before coming home. Astronauts could be on Mars for a couple of years, I guess."

"Right," Mei answered. "And the research on the International Space Station is sort of like a trial run, to see if the human body could handle it."

Hayato was curious now. "So what are they finding?"

"The astronauts up there suffer bone loss."

"What? How much are they losing?"

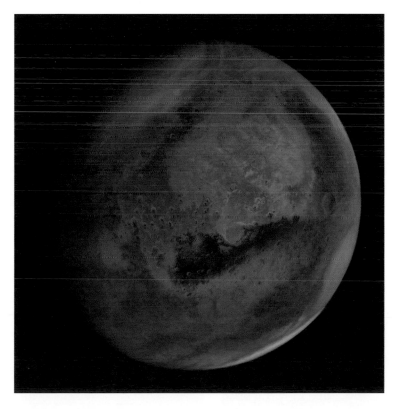

In 2014, NASA launched a space probe to Mars that may provide data that will help future manned missions.

"From what I read," Mei said, "they are losing about 10 percent over a six-month stay."

Hayato could see the problem. "Yikes. If it is a six-month trip to Mars then the astronauts could lose 10 percent of their bone mass before they even step on the planet."

"Exactly. That would mean that those astronauts would be at real risk of fractures and broken bones."

Hayato finished her thought " . . . and there might not be a doctor handy!"

Mei nodded. "See why the research on the International Space Station is so important? I read that it could take three or four years back home on Earth to recover from that bone loss."

Not Just Space

Research on the bone loss suffered by astronauts can help others on Earth, too. Treatments given to the astronauts to minimize this bone loss have real life implications for the elderly on Earth. The elderly lose 1–2 percent of their bone density each year. Studies in space can hopefully help prevent fractures in the elderly. While in space, astronauts exercise daily (below) to help prevent or slow this bone loss.

Try It Yourself

One of the dietary supplements given to astronauts on the International Space Station is calcium. Calcium helps make your bones strong. See what can happen to your bones if they don't get enough calcium.

Materials:
- 3 clean and dry chicken or turkey bones
- 3 glass jars
- vinegar
- water
- calcium powder

1. Fill each glass jar about ¾ of the way with water. Place 3 tablespoons of vinegar in one jar. Add 3 tablespoons of calcium powder to another, leaving the third unaltered.

2. Label each jar.

3. Add a chicken bone to each jar, making sure the bones are completely submerged in the water.

4. What do you think will happen to the bones in each jar? Write your predictions.

5. Wait a week. At the end of that time carefully remove the bones.

6. How do they feel? How do they look? What impact did the vinegar have on the bone? What about the calcium powder?

8
MAGLEV TRAINS

Hayato reached into his backpack and brought out a pamphlet he had picked up in the airport in Tokyo. It described the Chuo Shinkansen project. This was a new train planned to connect the cities of Tokyo, Nagoya, and Osaka. Traveling at speeds of up to 314 miles per hour (mph; or 505 kph), the entire trip by train would take less than two hours.

Hayato whistled under his breath. He looked over at Mei to tell her about this but saw that she was asleep. "Wow. 314 mph. How does that happen?"

"I did a report about this in social studies class," Mei said. "It's actually a pretty cool story."

"Wait a minute," Hayato interrupted. "Social studies? I thought you would learn about this in science class. What does super-fast train technology have to do with social studies?"

"The reason the engineers were able to have the money and the room to build the trains was because of what was happening in Japan after World War II," Mei began. "And because of how Japan's land is used and cities are built. The whole country is on islands. Nearly all of the places to live are along the edges of the islands. As the cities got bigger, people had to move farther and farther away. That meant they had to travel farther and farther back to their jobs in the cities. Japan was looking for ways to get those people to work faster. So they thought of fast trains."

"Okay, I get that, but how does World War II have anything to do with it?" Hayato asked.

"In the years after the war, many parts of Japan had to be rebuilt. With a fresh canvas to build on, Japan could start from scratch in some ways. One way was to create long, closed sections of land for railroads. If you have a very fast railroad, you don't want to have it cross roads or have to wait for cars to cross the tracks. So they needed a way to create pathways for the trains that would be on bridges or tunnels, over or under roads and water."

"So once they had all those tracks, they could put trains on them," Hayato said. "But where does the high-speed science come in. Oh, wait, I can actually help with that." He read further in the magazine.

Hayato read that high-speed trains use maglev, or magnetic levitation, technology. There are no wheels on the trains—they use magnets to hover on a specialized track. The track is called a guideway. When a powerful electric current is sent to both magnets, the magnets on the track repel the magnets on the bottom of the train. The magnets are set up so that the train hovers anywhere between 0.39 and 3.93 inches (1 to 10 cm) above the track.

"Well, now the thing is floating over the track. How does it move forward?" wondered Hayato to himself.

He read on and found the answer. Along the sides of the guideway are a series of coils. An electric current is fed into the coils. The current turns a magnetic field on and off. This creates a pull on the front of the train, and a push on the back of the train, which moves the train along.

Hayato learned that it is the lack of **friction** that allows the train to go so fast. The fact that the train is essentially floating on a cushion of

Words to Understand

friction the resistance encountered when an object rubs against another object or on a surface

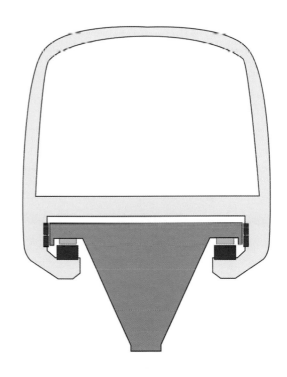

Magnets on the track (green) and on the train (red) are of opposite poles. When powered by electricity, they create a repelling force powerful enough to lift and move the train.

air makes it possible to reach such high speeds. These trains can travel about twice as fast as the fastest commuter train today. They started out as a solution to a crowded island population moving around, and have become a technological marvel. Speeds have only increased from the early days, and today, the "bullet" trains are the fastest in the world.

"It says here that the maglev train in Japan is the only commercial one in the world," Hayato said. "I can't believe we didn't see that when we were there. Now we have to come back. I want to ride on that train!" Hayato said to his sleeping sister.

A Maglev Heart?

Maglev technology is used for more than just transportation. The medical community has found uses for these magnets too. There is an experimental device for the heart, which uses maglev technology. The device (right) is about the size of a hockey puck and is placed inside a patient's chest and attached to their heart. It revolves, using maglev technology, to push blood from the heart out into the body. This technology is thought to be better than traditional mechanical pumps because it causes fewer dangerous blood clots.

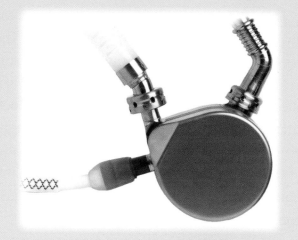

Try it Yourself

Make your own maglev.

Materials:
- shoe box
- 20 button magnets
- glue
- scissors
- small block of wood or plastic toy car

1. Identify the poles of the magnets. Do this by moving two magnets toward each other. If they are attracted, then the opposite poles of the magnet are facing. If they are repelled, then the poles are the same.

2. Arrange two rows of 8 magnets each along the inside of the shoe box. Be sure to place them so the same pole is facing up. Glue the magnets down.

3. Glue the remaining 4 magnets to the bottom of the plastic car or block of wood. Arrange them so they will sit directly over the magnets within the shoebox. Glue them so that the opposite pole is facing down.

4. Carefully place the wood over the track. What happens? What if you gently nudge the wood?

9
WRAPPING IT UP

Travel Science. It is hard to believe that something as fun, exciting, and eye opening as traveling can be related to science but it's true. All aspects of travel rely, at some point or another, on science. Whether you are traveling by car, bus, plane, train, or boat—at least one discipline of science helped you make the journey.

As science and technology have developed, so, too, has our ability to travel. Early Viking ships were propelled by oars. Explorers sailed the seas in sailing vessels powered by the wind and navigated by the stars. People around the world used to travel by horse, or covered wagon, and simply by foot.

Yet, look at what we have today. Today, you can fly around the world in an airplane in a matter of hours. Ships use sophisticated sonar technology and navigate with satellites orbiting Earth. Scientists and explorers travel to the deepest oceans and out into space. Trains rocket across the Earth at more than 250 miles (430 km) per hour. Never before have humans been able to move about on the Earth with such speed and ease.

This ease of travel does come with a price. The biggest cost is probably the environmental impact of travel. Airplanes and automobiles use fossil fuels to operate. Fossil fuels are nonrenewable resources that release gases into the atmosphere, which impact the global climate. Airplane travel leads to personal problems such as jet lag, inner ear issues, and blood clots. Astronauts traveling to space deal with bone loss and other issues related to being away from Earth's gravity. Underwater explorers are also faced with the challenges of extreme pressure and lack of oxygen.

Burning fuel spews out exhaust from billions of vehicles every day around the world. Travel extracts a price from the environment.

Flying in the sunset can make for beautiful pictures, but too much flying can actually affect your blood and your cells. Check it out!

Try this one last activity. Long plane rides—those that last more than four hours—can have some very strange effects on your body. It's not just a matter of jet lag. Do some research online to find out more. For example, flying in an airplane exposes a person to more radiation from the Sun than is typically found on the surface of Earth. This is because the atmosphere thins out at above 30,000 feet (about 9,000 m). The thinner atmosphere provides less protection from the radiation. A trip from New York to California will expose you to about as much radiation as you would get in a chest X-ray.

Next, research the impact that travel has on your blood, on your cells, and on your ears. Create a public service announcement explaining for people the realities of airplane travel. Be sure to include steps that they can take to lessen the effects. With every benefit of travel come risks and consequences. Knowing as much as you can about both sides of that coin will make you healthier.

As Mei and her brother Hayato flew across the Pacific, they pondered many topics related to travel—from the Coriolis effect to unsinkable ships to time zones. The next time you take a trip, whether it is across town or across the ocean, think about all that goes into making your trip possible.

Travel Science 24-7: Concept Review

Chapter 1
Airplanes are heavy machines that can carry people around the globe. Find out how they operate thanks to the same basic principles that allow birds to fly.

Chapter 2
Mei and Hayato find out how a ship stays afloat by using a glass of water and some ice cubes.

Chapter 3
Traveling across Europe requires a passport. It also requires you to change the time on your watch several times. This chapter looked at the time zones on Earth.

Chapter 4
Some airplane trips leave the passengers tired and groggy. Read all about jet lag in this chapter.

Chapter 5
Hayato and Mei found out why objects on Earth don't really travel in a straight path.

Chapter 6
Want to be an astronaut? Then this chapter about space travel might interest you.

Chapter 7
Space travel isn't all exciting, though. There are many changes that happen to the body while an astronaut is in space.

Chapter 8
A train that floats an inch off of the track? Is this science fiction? Or is it a technology that uses magnets to make super-fast trains?

FIND OUT MORE

Books

How exactly did the Wright brothers invent the airplane? Read all about it.
Freedman, Russell. *The Wright Brothers: How They Invented the Airplane.*
New York: Holiday House, 1994.

Want to learn more about maglev trains and what the trains of the future might look like?
Check out this book.
McMahon, Peter. *Ultimate Trains (Machines of the Future)*. Tonawanda, N.Y.: Kids Can Press,
2010.

Want to make some really neat paper airplanes while learning a little at the same time?
Try this book.
Stillinger, Doug. *Klutz Book of Paper Airplanes*. New York: KLUTZ, 2004.

Web Sites

What would it be like on the International Space Station? Take a tour of this Web site, set up
by NASA, to find out.
www.nasa.gov/audience/forstudents/dayinthelife/index.html

What time is it? Find out the time and date of any place in the world here on this Web site.
www.timeanddate.com/worldclock/

Want to know a little bit more about why boats float? Check this out.
www.scientificamerican.com/article/bring-science-home-how-metal-boats-float/

Series Glossary of Key Terms

alleles different forms of a gene; offspring inherit one allele from each parent

chromosomes molecules within an organism which contain DNA

climate change the ongoing process in which the temperature of the Earth is growing over time

force in science, strength or energy that comes as a result of a physical movement or action

frequency number of waves that pass a given point in a certain period of time

friction the resistance encountered when an object rubs against another object or on a surface

gene molecular unit of heredity of living organisms

gravity the force that pulls objects toward the ground

greenhouse gases gases in the atmosphere that trap radiation from the sun

inertia tendency of an object to resist change in motion

laser an intensified beam of light

lift the force that acts to raise a wing or an airfoil

momentum the amount of motion by a moving object

semiconductor a substance that has a conductivity between that of an insulator and that of most metals

sustainable able to be maintained at a certain rate or level

traits characteristics of an organism that are passed to the next generation

wavelength a measurement of light that is the distance from the top of one wave to the next

PICTURE CREDITS

Air New Zealand: 20
DCC Doppelmayr Cable Car : 37
Dollarphoto: Catmando 40
Dreamstime.com:
    Boarding1now: 8
    Ivan Cholakov: 12
    Bcreigh: 13
    Hypnocreative: 14
    Yakobchuk: 16
    Jorisvo: 21 left
    Songquam Deng: 21 right
    SolarSeven: 24
    Jelen80: 26
    Roza: 28
    Gas2: 36
    Gbp: 41
    Eugenef: 42

Markus Scheider: 30
NASA: 32 (ESA), 33, 34
Terumo Heart Inc./University of Michigan: 38
Utrecht University: 18

ABOUT THE AUTHOR

Jane P. Gardner has written more than a dozen books for young and young-adult readers on science and other nonfiction topics. She became an author after a career as a science educator. She lives in Massachusetts with her husband, two sons, plus a cat and a gecko!

ABOUT THE CONSULTANT

Russ Lewin has taught physics, robotics, astronomy, and math at Santa Barbara Middle School in California for more than 25 years. His creative and popular classes and curriculum include a hands-on approach to learning and exploring that instills a love of science in his students.

INDEX